istarif

THE OPEN MEDIA PAMPHLET SERIES

4

THE OPEN MEDIA PAMPHLET SERIES

Globalizing Civil Society
Reclaiming Our Right to Power

DAVID C. KORTEN

Series editors Greg Ruggiero and Stuart Sahulka

SEVEN STORIES PRESS / New York

A Seven Stories Press First Edition,
published in association with Open Media.

Open Media Pamphlet Series editors,
Greg Ruggiero and Stuart Sahulka.

Library of Congress Cataloging-in-Publication Data

Korten, David C.
    Globalizing civil society / David C. Korten. — 1st ed
    p.   cm. —(The Open Media Pamphlet Series)
    ISBN 1-888363-59-2
    1. Civil society. 2. Democracy. 3. International eco-
nomic relations. 4. Social justice. 5. Sustainable development. I. Title. II. Series.
JC336.K65 1997
301—DC21   97-23149
                                      CIP

Book design by Cindy LaBreacht

9 8 7 6 5 4 3 2 1

What is needed to provide healthy and sustainable living spaces for a growing world population on a finite planet? It is surely one of the most important questions of our time. Yet the institutions to which we have entrusted decision making power over the use of the world's resources are so focused on the promotion of expanded international trade and financial speculation that they scarcely seem to notice the rapidly deteriorating situation in much of the world with regard to the environment, human rights, food security, population, unemployment, poverty, and the social fabric. The evidence accumulates almost daily leading to the inescapable conclusion that our dominant institutions are not only failing, their favored policies are actively accelerating the deterioration. It is left to civil society to expose the causes of the institutional dysfunction and to define and pursue alternatives.

The search for these causes and alternatives has become a growing concern of activist groups and NGOs (non-governmental organizations) at every level of society and has unfolded into an expanding civil society dialogue. While the views of civil society are as diverse as its participants, a line of analysis has arisen from this dialogue that has a broad and growing base of support among people of widely varied backgrounds who share a deep concern for the future of our world. It presents a perspective seldom heard in official forums, perhaps because it is understandably difficult for those who represent official institutions to engage in public discussion of issues that bear on the legitimacy of the institutions they represent.

I have been an active participant in the unfolding civil society dialogue and my own thinking has been deeply influenced by it. This Open Media Pamphlet presents my personal interpretation and articulation of the emerging analysis, and is based on the UN sponsored Habitat II Conference held in Istanbul in June, 1996. The analysis represents a significant departure from the accepted world view that currently informs most public policy discussions and helps explain why the resulting policies so often fail. For example, it suggests that:

➤ The major barriers to providing healthy and sustainable living spaces for a growing world population are institutional rather than financial and corrective action must be guided by a theory of why our present institutions are failing. Without such a theory, attention tends to focus on funding programs that treat the symptoms of failure to the neglect of their underlying causes. The resulting actions are almost inevitably overly expensive, fragmented, incomplete, often contradictory, and ineffectual.

➤ To move toward the creation of a world of just and sustainable human societies, we must move beyond many twentieth century ideas and institutions not appropriate to our current historical reality. The persistence of the problems addressed by the series of UN conferences now completed should be viewed as a warning sign telling us that these values and institutions are leading us where no sane person wants to go and that adjustments at the margin are unlikely to be adequate.

➤ Most human needs can be met only through appropriate local action. One reason appropriate action is not forthcoming is because of policy actions that concentrate control over productive resources in institutions that are unmindful of local needs and lack public accountability for the consequences of their actions. Enabling action is needed at global and national levels to restore to local people and communities control of the productive assets on which their livelihoods depend.

The purpose of this pamphlet is to engage the public in an open dialogue that places these issues on the table for serious examination and action.

I. Beyond the Legacies of the Twentieth Century

The twentieth century has been a period of profound contradictions—at once a time of extraordinary human advancement and a time of deepening crisis. In one century our species has achieved greater advance in technology and the ability to create and manage powerful globe-spanning organizations than were achieved in thousands of years of prior history. Yet even with the enormous capabilities now at hand, human societies are gripped by a rapidly deepening crisis of social disintegration, economic inequality, and environmental unsustainability. As most elements of the crisis have been given wide public visibility, it would serve little purpose to further document them here. Of more immediate concern is the troubling reality that the dominant thrust of policy action and resource allocation decision-making in the world continues in a business-as-usual mode—almost as if the crisis that manifests itself in so many ways either does not exist or is a matter of secondary importance.

There is an explanation for this puzzling paradox that leads to useful insights into the deeper nature and causes of the crisis itself.

SUCCESS IN THE MONEY WORLD, CRISIS IN THE LIVING WORLD

During the latter part of the second millennium, and in particular the twentieth century, the lives of most of the world's people have become increasingly divided between two parallel and intertwined realities. One reality—the world of money—is governed by the rules set by governments and central banks and by the dynamics of financial markets. The other—the world of life—is governed by the laws of nature.[1]

In the world of money, the health of society and its institutions is measured by financial and economic indicators—by growth in such things as economic output, stock prices, trade, investment, and tax receipts. In the world of money, continuous, sustained growth seems to be the primary imperative. Because they are structured to seek ever-increasing productivity and profits, modern economies either grow in terms of the monetary value of their output, or they collapse. The growth imperative of the money world finds expression in the notion of development as an unending process of economic expansion—which has been the organizing principle of public policy for most of the last half of this century.

The living world is governed by quite different imperatives. Here healthy function manifests itself in balance,

DAVID C. KORTEN

diversity, sufficiency, synergy, and regenerative vitality. Growth is an integral part of the living world, but only as a clearly defined segment of the life cycle of individual organisms. The sustained physical growth of any individual organism or unlimited numerical expansion of any species is an indicator of system dysfunction and poses a threat to system integrity. Thus growth in the living world tends to be self-limiting—as with a cancer that condemns its host or a species whose numbers upset the ecological balance and ultimately destroy its food supply.

Though as living beings we are creatures of the living world, we have yielded the power of decision in human affairs to the institutions of the money world and for these institutions the imperatives of the world of money take precedence over those of the living world. Money-world institutions have been enormously successful in shaping the twentieth century's advances in technical and organizational mastery as instruments of economic growth. Indeed they have increased total world economic output from five to seven times over the past fifty years. They have also brought unprecedented material wealth to approximately 20 percent of the world's people and vast riches to the most fortunate one percent. The world's power holders, who with few exceptions belong to the most fortunate one percent, understandably see this as a considerable accomplishment. Having experienced the possibilities of the underlying development model, they feel affirmed in their belief that the systems of governance that allocate the world's resources are fundamentally sound. Shielded by their wealth from sharing in the living-world consequences of money-world decisions, those consequences lack—for them—a compelling sense of reality.

From the perspective of the living world, however, the consequences of the economic development/growth agenda have been disastrous. Here we see that each addition to economic output results in a comparable increase in the stress that humans place on the earth's ecosystem, deepens the poverty of those whose resources have been expropriated and labor exploited to fuel the engines of growth, and accelerates the destruction of nonhuman species. The terrible costs fall on those who are denied a political voice—the poor, the young, and generations yet unborn.

Most of the benefit of increased economic output is going to those who already enjoy a substantial level of physical comfort and security—contributing more to an increase in inequality than to a reduction in poverty. A single statistic reveals how obscene inequality has become. In 1996 the world had 447 billionaires, up from 274 in 1991. Their combined net worth equals the estimated combined annual income of the poorest half of humanity. Denied both a political voice and economic opportunity, the excluded are often left with crime and violence as their only evident avenues for survival, self-expression, and individual advancement.

Violence in the home and in the streets has become a pervasive part of the human experience. We must consider what must be done to address unmet needs for human shelter, community, and livelihoods. Military conflicts—sponsored by some of the same governments and supplied by a flourishing international arms trade— are systematically destroying existing housing stocks, communities, and livelihoods in campaigns of terror and genocide. The landmines that are but one legacy of these conflicts will render vast areas of desperately needed land

DAVID C. KORTEN

unsafe for habitation or cultivation for decades to come. Such armed conflicts are a primary cause of an alarming increase in the number of refugees in the world. In 1960, the UN listed 1.4 million international refugees. By 1992, the number had grown to 18.2 million. The UN estimates that currently an additional 24 million people are displaced within the borders of their own countries.[2]

No less tragic is the suffering of the tens of millions of development refugees, the victims of the silent violence of development projects that expropriate—and often destroy—their homes, lands, waters, and fisheries for uses such as hydroelectric dams, tree plantations, and urban development projects that often benefit fewer people—usually better off—than those they displace. These development refugees are deprived of shelter, community, and means of livelihood just as certainly as are the victims of organized armed violence.

The evidence is mounting. Despite impressive increases in average life spans, a major portion of humanity has gained little benefit—and in many instances suffered considerable loss—from the economic prosperity that has brought unimaginable wealth to a few. In short, while the long term trends in the money world point toward ever-increasing prosperity, the long-term trends in the living world point to growing imbalance, instability, and system stress. Dealing with this reality is basic to any effort to create socially and environmentally sustainable human settlements.

In large measure, the crisis of global-scale social and environmental disintegration now underway can be explained in terms of a confrontation between the conflicting imperatives of the money world—which holds the power of decision—and the living world of people and nature—which bears the tragic consequences of those decisions.

UNDERLYING CAUSES OF SYSTEM FAILURE

In substantial measure the policies responsible for the imbalance are a legacy of twentieth century ideas and institutions that go largely unchallenged by those who have been their primary beneficiaries. Government officials, policy experts, corporate representatives, and official declarations continuously reaffirm, almost as an article of religious faith, a belief that economic growth, market deregulation, privatization, and economic "globalization" are the irreducible foundations of peace, equality, human rights, democracy, a healthy environment and social fabric, and universal prosperity. From the perspective of the money world, the logic of such assertions is impeccable. From the perspective of the living world the logic suffers from three serious flaws:

➤ Continued economic growth on a finite planet with an already overtaxed ecosystem accelerates environmental breakdown, intensifies the competition for resources between rich and poor, and deprives future generations of the necessary means to meet their basic needs. This is confirmed by a growing body of evidence that many of the world's ocean fisheries, fresh water resources, and farm and forest lands are being exploited at rates substantially greater than their ability to regenerate.[3]

➤ Expansion of the market economy ever more activities once performed by households and communities is monetizing human relationships, weakening the social

DAVID C. KORTEN

fabric, and destroying livelihoods faster than jobs offering, more than poverty-level compensation are being created.

➤ The institutions of a globalized, free market economy that control privatized assets respond only to the imperatives of the money world. They are virtually blind to the imperatives of the living world. Economic globalization is shifting control over resources, markets, and technology from people, communities, and governments to transnational financial markets and corporations—placing these institutions beyond the reach of public accountability, making responsible local action to meet local needs increasingly difficult, and creating dangerous financial instability.

A free market allocates fairly and efficiently only when market players have equal economic power. When extreme economic inequality is combined with market deregulation, the rich invariably win the competition for scarce resources—with results that are neither fair, nor efficient. The wealthy become ever more powerful, gain control of the rule-making system, and accelerate the process of rewriting society's rules to their own advantage. Social services used by the jobless and the working poor are cut back in the name of fiscal responsibility. Tax structures become more regressive as subsidies and tax breaks are granted to the most wealthy investors in the name of job creation. Regulatory restraints on the concentration and abuse of corporate power are relaxed. Such agendas are being advanced by elite interests all over the world—by right wing political movements in the North and through structural adjustment programs implemented by the World Bank and the International Monetary Fund (IMF) in the South.

One of the challenges to colonial administrators was that many colonized people obtained their livelihoods from their own lands and common areas. For colonists to profit from the lands, labor, and consumption of subjected people it was necessary to force them into dependence on a money economy. This was accomplished by such measures as limiting access to common lands by declaring all "uncultivated" lands property of the colonial administration and by imposing taxes payable only in cash.

In many parts of the world this played into a process of deepening gender-differentiated economic roles—with men most often specializing in paid employment in the money economy, confining women to serving a wide range of essential—but inadequately valued—household and community productive and reproductive needs in what remained of the nonmonetized "social economy." During the past ten to twenty years there have been dramatic economic changes in many countries. Declining wages, cutbacks in public services for the poor, and a rise in single parenting have made women more dependent on their personal earnings from the money economy—often in petty trade or insecure jobs under substandard conditions. There has not, however, been a compensating reduction in the maintenance needs of households and communities for unpaid work. With neither men nor women able to give adequate attention to those nonmonetized household and community functions that maintain the social fabric of society, relationships of trust and caring have been giving way to fear and violence as revealed in the growth in violent crime, spouse abuse, divorce, teenage suicide, and drug use being experienced around the world.

DAVID C. KORTEN

CONCENTRATING POWER, SHEDDING ACCOUNTABILITY

A combination of economic globalization and productivity-enhancing technology continue to transform economic relations in ways that add to widespread inequality and instability. Trade agreements negotiated under the General Agreement on Tariffs and Trade (GATT), the structural adjustment policies of the World Bank and International Monetary Fund (IMF), and advances in communications technology are melding national economies into a seamless global economy. Transnational corporations are more able to shift the production to localities that offer lower production costs without fear of losing access to more affluent markets. At the same time, advanced information technologies are making it possible for a small fraction of the potential workforce to produce most of the goods and services the global marketplace is able to absorb. The U.S. *Fortune 500* industrial corporations reduced their total employment by 4.4 million jobs between 1980 and 1993—a period during which their sales increased by 1.4 times, assets by 2.3 times, and CEO compensation by 6.1 times.[4]

While the giants are shedding people, they are not shedding control over money, markets, or technology. The world's 200 largest industrial corporations, which employ only one-third of the world's population, control 28 percent of the world's economic output.[5] The top 300 transnationals, excluding financial institutions, own some 25 percent of the world's productive assets.[6] Of the world's 100 largest economies, 51 are now corporations—not including banking and financial institutions. The combined assets of the world's 50 largest commercial banks and diversified financial companies amount to nearly 60 percent of *The Economist's* estimate of a $20 trillion global stock of productive capital.[7]

Concentration of control over markets is proceeding apace. *The Economist* recently reported that in the consumer durables industry the top five firms control *nearly 70 percent* of the entire world market, a ratio that economists consider highly monopolistic. In the automotive, airline, aerospace, electronic components, electrical and electronics, and steel industries the top five firms control more than 50 percent of the global market, placing them clearly in the category of monopolistic industries. In the oil, personal computers and media industries the top five firms control more than 40 percent of sales, which indicates strong monopolistic tendencies.[8] Yet the consolidation continues with no end in sight. The total value of mergers and acquisitions completed worldwide during 1995 was expected to reach $800 billion—exceeding the total for any previous year by more than 25 percent.[9]

The same firms shedding employees while tightening control over capital and markets are also shedding their obligation to provide good wages and working conditions for those who produce the goods and services they sell. The popular Nike athletic shoes that sell for US $73 to $135 around the world are produced by 75,000 workers employed by independent contractors in low income countries. A substantial portion of these workers are in Indonesia—mostly women and girls housed in company barracks, paid as little as 15 cents an hour, and required to work mandatory overtime. Unions are forbidden and strikes are broken up by the military. In 1992, Michael Jordan reportedly received $20 million from the

DAVID C. KORTEN

Nike corporation to promote the sale of its shoes, more than the total compensation paid to the Indonesian women who made them.[10] An unregulated global market is shifting the financial rewards away from those who produce what others need to those who control money and are successful at convincing others to buy what they neither need nor can afford.

The living world cries out for more cooperation among localities toward the creation of higher social and environmental standards. Yet people and communities on opposite sides of the globe are pitted against one another in a desperate global competition for the available jobs by outdoing one another in courting corporate favor by offering ever more attractive subsidies and tax holidays, lower wages, and lax environmental and employment standards.

THE GLOBAL CASINO

The corporations that are the most visible players in this global "race for the bottom" are themselves captive to the dynamics of a *world* financial system that gives them little freedom to manage their affairs with the broader public interest in mind. More than $1 trillion changes hands each day in the world's international currency markets—seeking short-term financial returns unrelated to the production or trade of any actual goods or services.

The globalized financial system has become a giant gambling casino in which the players are betting on short-term fluctuations in the prices of financial instruments in search of instant gains unrelated to productive contribution. Such gains are almost inherently extractive, meaning that they make no consequential contribution to adding value to any real product. They depend on extracting wealth from others who are doing productive work and making real long-term investment in the production of needed goods and services. The players in these markets operate in a virtual reality of cyberspace, a world of pure money wholly detached from the living world and blind to its imperatives.

Of course currency traders are a minority of the professionals who manage the investment pools controlled by large investment houses, banks, mutual funds, and retirement funds. The dynamics are similar, however, even with those whose trades involve stocks and bonds that represent ownership shares in real companies. Whether their decisions contribute to creating real goods and services that people want and need is not their concern. The pressures for instant gains encourage excesses that make the entire financial system increasingly unstable. This instability and its real world consequences were starkly revealed in the Mexican pesos crisis of December 1994.

Until the moment of the crash, Mexico was being touted as an economic miracle. Yet what looked like a dynamic economy was mainly an illusion created by Mexico's success in attracting $70 billion in foreign money over five years with high interest bonds and a super-heated stock market. As little as 10 percent of this money went into real investment.[11] Most of it financed consumer imports, capital flight, and debt service payments. It also helped to create 24 Mexican billionaires.[12] The bubble burst in December 1994 as the hot money rushed out. Mexico's stock market and the value of the peso plummeted. The subsequent Mexican austerity pol-

DAVID C. KORTEN

icy and a shifting terms of trade between the United States and Mexico resulted in massive job losses on both sides of the border. U.S. President Clinton responded by putting together a $50 billion bailout package at taxpayer expense to assure that the Wall Street firms that held Mexican bonds would be repaid. The new link between the dollar and the peso made currency speculators nervous and the value of the dollar fell sharply against the yen. Not a penny of the bailout money went to 750,000 Mexicans who would be put out of work by government imposed austerity measures.[13] Subsequent financial failures in Thailand, Malaysia, Indonesia, the Phillipines, South Korea, and Brazil followed similar patterns. And like Mexico, they elicited a commitment of billions of dollars in public money to protect the foreign bankers.

More than any other human institution, the global financial system in which hundreds of billions of dollars move unimpeded across national borders at the first hint of changing financial prospects is setting the world's social and economic priorities. Yet the social and environmental consequences of the actions for which the major players in that system reap handsome rewards, never register on their computer screens.

As evidence mounts of the failure of our mega-institutions to deal with two of the most fundamental requirements of healthy social function—economic justice and environmental sustainability—fear, disillusionment, and distrust increase and the legitimacy of these institutions erodes. This opens the way to growing political extremism and instability and creates a fertile ground for demagogues who build their political base on foundations of ethnic, racial, and religious hatred and violence. The resulting social breakdown is already well advanced in many parts of the world—most particularly in Africa and many inner cities of both North and South. Until the underlying institutional causes of growing injustice and unsustainable exploitation of the ecosystem are addressed, the crises will almost certainly continue to deepen.

PREPARING FOR A NEW ERA

In dealing with the conflicting imperatives of money and life we face an inescapable reality that both economists and environmentalists commonly overlook. While the money world is our creation, we are creatures of the living world. Money is a useful means of facilitating certain kinds of transactions among people—nothing more. It is the living world that gave us birth and sustains us in life. Money must be the servant of life, not its master.

Money-world institutions are human creations, and it is within our power to reconstruct them in ways that align their imperatives with the imperatives of living. As we lack the option of changing the rules of the living world to align with the imperatives of the money world, the institutions of money must therefore be reconstructed to serve the needs of people and life.

Justice and sustainability will need to become the organizing principles of public policy. Acting in our citizen roles, we must give meaning to the democratic principle of citizen sovereignty by reclaiming the power we have yielded to the institutions of global finance and returning it to the small and local—institutions of people and community securely rooted in the living world.

The first step in producing a comprehensive agenda for the creation of just and sustainable societies is to

DAVID C. KORTEN

bring together the institutions of civil society and government to engage the process of building an agenda for a life-centered reconstruction of human societies.

Ultimately this agenda-building process must address three needs:

➤ The need to organize human habitats in ways that support the right of all people to a place in society and on the earth with access to the resources required to create a secure and fulfilling life for themselves at peace with their neighbors and in balance with the earth's natural systems.

➤ The need to build—as complementary to the money economy—strong gender-balanced nonmonetized household and community economies able to replenish the social capital that is essential to healthy and efficient function of both economies and societies.

➤ The need to create a global system of localized economies that root economic power and environmental responsibility in people and communities of place and encourage a substantial measure of local environmental self-reliance.

Effective action on these needs is out of step with the prevailing conventional wisdom of economic policy which is taking us in the wrong direction. Our future depends on making a significant and conscious course change.

It is a timely moment to initiate a global process of reflection, envisioning, and institutional renewal. The year 2000 is rapidly approaching to mark our passage from the second to the third millennium. This rare anniversary offers an opportunity to focus the emergent social and political energies of an awakening global civil society on building and advancing citizen agendas responsive to new needs and potentials.

The stage has been set for such an undertaking by the conjunction of a compelling need, the rapid expansion of global communications facilities, a capacity to organize ourselves in large-scale, non-hierarchical networks, and the emergence of a new global consciousness of the inherent interdependence of all life. For the first time in the history of our species, the possibility exists to engage virtually everyone in a collective process of reflecting on the meaning of the human experience and creating and acting upon a bold and visionary agenda for the informed and intentional creation of our own future.

While such an undertaking must build on the successes of our collective past, it must also involve a willingness to move beyond those 20th century ideas and institutions that now stand in the way of humanity taking the step to greater moral and spiritual maturity.

II. Guiding Principles for the Third Millenium

An essential first step toward giving precedence to the imperatives of the living world is to recognize that our challenge for the third millennium is not to accelerate and sustain economic growth—which is a money-world imperative—but rather to create just, sustainable, and democratic societies that bring the human species into balance with itself and the planet—a living-world imperative. These three essential characteristics of healthy societies—just, sustainable, and democratic—align with three guiding principles: equity, sustainability, and civic engagement. Each of these principles

DAVID C. KORTEN

addresses a basic underlying cause of the larger crisis. Together they provide an essential framework for corrective action.

The following elaboration of the original principles may help to demonstrate their central importance.

THE PRINCIPLE OF SUSTAINABILITY

To be sustainable, a human economy must not place greater demands on the ecosystem than what the ecosystem can sustain through its natural regenerative processes. In other words, the economy must meet the needs of present generations while maintaining itself in balance with the ecosystem. According to Herman Daly, sustainability is accomplished only when three basic conditions are met.

➤ Rates of use of renewable resources must not exceed the rates at which the ecosystem is able to regenerate them;

➤ Rates of consumption or irretrievable disposal of nonrenewable resources must not exceed the rate at which renewable substitutes are developed and phased into use;

➤ Rates of pollution emission into the environment must not exceed the rates of the ecosystem's natural assimilative capacity.[14]

Any use of environmental resources or sink capacities greater than these rates is by definition unsustainable and compromises the opportunities available to future generations—raising an important issue of intergenerational equity. Since mid-century, aggregate economic output has increased from five to seven times—with corresponding increases in the demands human activities place on the environment. As a consequence, aggregate human uses of the environment already exceed sustainable rates in many areas and are rapidly approaching them in most others.

The first environmental limits that we have confronted, and in some instances exceeded, are not the limits to nonrenewable resource exploitation, as many once anticipated, but rather the limits to our use of renewable resources and the environment's sink functions—its ability to absorb our wastes. These are limits related to the depletion of soils, fisheries, forests, and water sources, to the absorption of CO_2 emissions, and to destruction of the ozone layer. The details of whether a particular limit was hit two years ago or will be passed by the turn of the century are far less important than coming to terms with the basic reality that for most practical purposes the consumption of our species has already expanded to fill or exceed the planet's available environmental space. It is time to get on with the task of adjusting our societies to this reality—including reexamining the criteria by which we judge economic performance.

THE PRINCIPLE OF EQUITY

While the use of economic growth as the measure of economic performance makes impeccable sense in terms of the imperatives of the money world, the more valid indicator from the perspective of the living world is whether an economy provides all its members those things essential to a healthy, secure, productive, and fulfilling life while using no more than each person's rightful share of the ecosystem's sustainable regenerative

DAVID C. KORTEN

productive capacity. Few, if any, economies currently meet this standard and there is ample evidence that economic growth is not the path to its attainment.

The ecosystem that gives us life is a living-world creation—a resource that is a common heritage of all living creatures. A right of access to a sufficient share of air, water, and land to sustain one's life is perhaps the most basic of human rights, tantamount to the right to exist—to have a place in society and on the earth to live, to find shelter and produce a livelihood.

What makes this a controversial issue is the fact that in a full world one person's right to a means of living regularly conflicts with the private property rights of another. There is no simple way to resolve this conflict, but it is essential to acknowledge it. In a world of increasing inequality, the legitimacy of institutions that give precedence to the property rights of "the Haves" over the human rights of "the Have Nots" is inevitably called into serious question. This suggests that there is need to distinguish between the property rights of those who have only that property required to meet their own needs and the property rights of persons and corporations whose holdings both exceed their own needs and deprive others of their means of living. Where property is equitably distributed, the protection of property rights represents a protection of one's right to a means of living. When property is owned by the few, property rights are too often used to legitimate denying others the right to live.

The most critical manifestation of this issue centers on rights of access to land and water. Both are fundamental to sustaining life and both are the objects of increasingly intense competition. Resolving this issue is one of the more complex and difficult issues to be faced in creating the legal and ethical foundations of just and sustainable societies.

Three recent studies of the relationship between population, consumption, and the limits of the environment's regenerative capacities provide a sobering perspective on how central, in questions of justice and sustainability, the conflict between property rights and human rights has become.

Ecological Footprints. A study by William Rees, an urban planner at the University of British Colombia, estimates that four to six hectares of land are required to maintain the consumption of the average person of a high income country. This estimate includes the land required to maintain current levels of energy consumption using renewable sources. Rees refers to the amount of productive land required to sustain the consumption of a particular urban population as its ecological footprint.

In 1990, the total available ecologically-productive land area (land capable of generating consequential biomass) in the world was an estimated 1.7 hectares per capita.[15] This suggests that the people of the high income industrial countries are running at a substantial ecological deficit. This is covered in part by the unsustainable drawing down of their own natural resource stocks and in part by expropriating the productive environmental output of the land areas of lower income countries. The latter is accomplished through patterns of international trade and investment that advantage the economically stronger party and lead to a global extension of its claims to property rights over ever more of the world's productive resources.

On a per capita basis, the United States and Canada are the world's most profligate consumers. Europe and Japan, however, have higher population densities in relation to their national land and resources and are thus generally living even farther beyond their own ecological means. Rees estimates that the population of the Netherlands, for example, consumes the output equivalent of some 14 times as much productive land as is contained within its own borders.[16] It makes up the deficit, as do most other deficit countries, by drawing down natural capital at the expense of future generations and appropriating the resources of others through international trade.

Equitable Sustainable Shares. A study by Friends of the Earth Netherlands has taken such analysis a step further by asking: What would be the allowable annual levels of consumption of environmental resources and waste absorption services for the average Dutch person in the year 2010, if: a) resource consumption levels were equal among all people living on the earth at that time and b) the global level of resource consumption is within sustainable limits? They then compared the results with current consumption levels in the Netherlands.[17] Friends of the Earth USA applied the Dutch estimates to make similar comparisons for the United States.[18]

The results are sobering.

Per capita annual CO_2 emissions are 19.5 tons in the United States and 12 tons in the Netherlands. To avoid global warming, world average per capita CO_2 emission levels from fossil fuel must drop to no more than 4 tons by 2010. Sharing this burden equally, in 2010 each person would be limited to consuming no more than 1 liter of carbon-based fuel per day. A Dutch person might chose between traveling 24 km (15.5 mi) by car, 50 km (31 mi) by bus, 65 km (40 mi) by train or 10 km (6.2 mi) by plane per day. A flight from Amsterdam to Rio de Janeiro, say to attend a gathering like the Earth Summit, could be taken only once every 20 years—assuming no other fossil fuel dependent travel during that period.[19]

While this might seem luxurious to those who now travel only by foot, it is sobering indeed for those of us who spend much of our lives in cars, planes, buses, and trains. Even more sobering is the realization that our allowance of one liter of fossil fuel a day must cover not only direct personal travel, but as well the production, transport, and marketing of the things we consume—our less visible burdens on the environment.

If we assume no more logging of primary forests and limit our use of wood products to wood harvested sustainably from existing non-primary forest lands, we could consume only 0.4 cubic meters per person per year—including the wood used to make paper. This would require a 79 percent reduction in timber consumption for the United States—and a 60 percent reduction for the Netherlands.

Balancing Population and Consumption. In a paper presented at the annual meeting of the American Association for the Advancement of Science, Cornell University Professor David Pimentel and his colleagues took the analysis a step further by looking at interactions among resource trade-offs and taking population as a variable. They noted, for example, that while it may be possible to raise more food by cultivating more land, this would require more water—which in many regions is scarcer than land. To get more of our energy from the

DAVID C. KORTEN

sun, we would need to convert land from food and fibre to energy production. To increase agricultural yields per hectare would require using more energy inputs from fossil fuels.

They ask the tough, but inescapable question, "Does human society want 10 to 15 billion humans living in poverty and malnourishment or one to two billion living with abundant resources and a quality environment?"[20] By their account the planet can only sustainably support one to two billion people at a per capita level of consumption comparable to that of Western Europe. They observe that "a drastic demographic adjustment to one to two billion humans will cause serious social economic, and political problems, but to continue rapid population growth to 12 billion or more will result in more severe social, economic, and political conflicts plus catastrophic public health and environmental problems."[21] As starkly as they present the choices, their study is probably overly optimistic as it addresses only human needs and allocates environmental space for only the animal and plant life devoted to direct human use.

While the Pimentel study is flawed by its acceptance of the prevailing myth that high levels of consumption and a high quality of life are synonymous, it compels us to face painful trade-offs that most discussions of overconsumption, population, and equity avoid. Pimentel, however, offers only two alternatives: universal high consumption lifestyles for a small population, or shared poverty with a large population. This overlooks a third option: organizing ourselves so that a population of five to six billion can enjoy a high quality of living with a moderate level of consumption (elaborated in Chapter 4 on Material Foundations of Just and Sustainable Societies).

The kinds of calculations presented in the three studies outlined above are at best preliminary approximations based on controversial assumptions and the use of fragmented and often unreliable data. However, this kind of unflinching look at the relationships between population, consumption, equity, and environmental limits is essential to any meaningful discussion of the human future. It is time to move beyond pointless debates about whether the problem is over-consumption in the North or population growth in the South. We must put aside the dangerous illusion that there is no need for redistribution because economic growth will eliminate poverty by making everyone richer, acknowledging that there are necessary limits to property rights, because in a full and unequal world there can be neither justice nor sustainability without rights of access for everyone to the means of livelihood.

THE PRINCIPLE OF CIVIC ENGAGEMENT

Civic engagement has many elements, but in its most basic sense it is about decision making, or governance, and about who and how and by whom a community's resources will be allocated. The principle of civic engagement underscores the most basic principle of democratic governance, i.e., that sovereignty resides ultimately in the people—in the citizenry. It is about the right of people to define the public good, determine the policies by which they will seek that good, and reform or replace institutions that do not serve that good.

Civic engagement goes to the heart of the question of whether money-world or living-world imperatives will prevail. Will decision processes be controlled exclusively by the few whose allegiance is to the imperatives of the

DAVID C. KORTEN

money world? Or will people struggling to survive in the context of the living world have a consequential voice? Will resource control be in the hands of financiers who see the world's cities and towns primarily as places from which to extract profits? Or by those who see them as places for living? Broadly-based civic participation does not guarantee wise public choices, but it does strengthen the voice of those who bear the living-world consequences of money-world policy choices.

The importance of the difference is illustrated by the following example of two very different ways a country might address its need for housing.

• **Option 1:** A country might obtain an international loan, perhaps from a commercial lender or the World Bank, and use the proceeds to import building materials and construction equipment and hire foreign construction contractors. Local laborers would receive temporary jobs and housing needs would be met quickly. However, the costs would be substantial, there would be little sustained impact on the local economy, and the country would eventually be required to boost its exports to repay its debt to foreign bankers.

• **Option 2:** Alternatively, a country might encourage local banks to make funds available for small housing construction loans. It could provide entrepreneurial and technical training, supporting services, and other incentives to encourage the formation of small firms to produce door frames, bricks, basic plumbing and electrical fixtures, and to provide construction contracting services. Government might subsidize research on the use of local materials to provide safe, affordable, and energy efficient housing. Housing and construction codes might be revised accordingly to favor use of local materials and labor-intensive construction methods. With this option, those in need get housing, plus new skills, new economic power, and new sources of livelihood. A system is in place to build and maintain the housing as required. And there is no new foreign debt to repay.

The technologies and materials involved in low-income housing are fairly basic and well within the means of most countries. There should be little need for foreign exchange. The first option favors the interests of the wealthy who control international construction firms and can benefit from the country's need to export to repay loans. The second option favors the interests of people working to create communities and livelihoods—essentials of healthy living. Engaging the people who need both houses and sources of livelihood in the decision process as part of a lively public debate will not assure a choice for option 2, but it will almost certainly increase its likelihood.

A substantial portion of new housing in low income countries is already being provided by the informal sector. Because informal housing construction is both more labor intensive and less costly than formal sector housing production, a given unit of housing expenditure in the informal sector produces both more jobs and more housing than comparable expenditure in the formal sector.[22]

The poor are among the most resourceful of the world's people. If there is a way to meet their needs, they will find generally it. A lack of housing is more often a consequence of a lack of access to the land, credit, and materials with which to create needed shelter than a lack of motivation or resourcefulness on their part.

DAVID C. KORTEN

Implementing land reform, providing secure titles to land, removing restrictions on using available local materials for constructon, and making credit available are often the most direct routes to meeting housing needs. Many housing needs may be met simply by reforming zoning and building codes to support the informal housing sector, encouraging the use of local building materials to which the informal sector is likely to have ready access, and facilitating incremental construction involving the addition of adding rooms and amenities—such as a tin roof.

This discussion of housing points to a larger truth. Most elements of the global crisis of deepening poverty, environmental destruction, and social disintegration can be satisfactorily resolved only through creative and committed local action by people working on the ground to create more satisfactory living places for themselves and their loved ones—household by household and community by community. The most pressing unmet needs of the world's people are food security, adequate shelter, clothing, health care, and education—the lack of which define true deprivation. With rare exception, the basic resources and capacity to meet these needs on a sustainable basis are already found in nearly every country.

Since the beginning of history, humans have organized themselves in tribes and villages that have found ways to use available resources and technologies to grow food, obtain water, construct shelter from available local materials, and treat their ailments. This heritage demonstrates that such forms of civic engagement are among the most natural and pervasive of human drives. The traditional ways of organizing community resources to meet human needs were substantially disrupted by the historical processes of industrialization and urbanization. Yet the pervasive efforts at self-help organization within urban neighborhoods and squatter communities demonstrates the persistence, pervasiveness, and importance of this drive.

Monetized economies tend to replace families and communities with markets, replace pathways where people meet with roadways where they isolate themselves in personal automobiles, and redefine the active citizen as passive consumer. In these and other ways, modernization tends to suppress the natural drive toward civic engagement. As that drive has declined, the power to govern has passed from people to distant institutions driven primarily by the imperatives of the money world. To create local habitats that serve their needs, people will need to reclaim that power and restore the rightful and necessary governance role of civil society.

Those whom the money world excludes live close to the realities of the living world. Corrective action must be informed by their experience and insights and by their natural motivation to create healthy places for living. A necessary step in creating just and sustainable societies is providing spaces for their voices to be heard and in drawing attention to the need for policies and institutions that enable local people and communities to regain control of their own resources and the direction of their lives.

III. Political and Economic Foundations of Just and Sustainable Societies

Markets and trade have essential roles in a world of just and sustainable societies. It must be clear, however, that they have no legitimate function other than as means to meet human needs. In the end, the most important test of the legitimacy and performance of any economy is the extent to which it assures the right of every person to a means of livelihood adequate to support full and healthy living. To meet this test, markets must be accountable to all people, not simply those with the most money. This means that markets and trade must both function within a framework of rules established and enforced by open, democratically accountable governments.

DEMOCRATIC PLURALISM

A struggle between two extremist ideologies has been a central feature of the twentieth century. Communism called for all power to the state. Market capitalism calls for all power to the market—which in a globalized economy means rule by global corporations and financial markets. Both ideologies lead to the concentration of power in distant and unaccountable institutions.

In the heat of ideological discourse it is easy to overlook the fact that the secret of Western success after World War II was not a reliance on free markets. It was a reliance on markets that functioned within strong regulatory frameworks administered by democratically accountable governments. The result was a system that was both more democratic and more pluralistic than either the communist or capitalist models.

Those who celebrate the fall of the planned economy in favor of the "free" market neglect the fact that the economy internal to a corporation is a planned economy—planned specifically to maximize corporate profits for the benefit of corporate owners. In an unregulated, globalized economy, the largest global corporations enjoy unprecedented freedom to insulate themselves from the discipline of market competition through mergers and strategic alliances that allow them to continuously increase their monopolistic control over markets, technology, resources, and money. The result is a concentration of economic power that is neither efficient nor democratic.

Contrary to commonly heard claims, markets need governments to function efficiently. It is well established in economic theory and practice that markets allocate resources efficiently only when they are competitive and individual firms internalize the full social and environmental costs of their production. Since successful firms invariably grow larger and more monopolistic, governments must regularly step in to break them up and restore competition. Similarly, since externalizing costs is a major source of significant competitive advantage, there is tremendous pressure on individual firms to do so to the full extent that public regulatory processes will allow.

As Herman Daly and John Cobb point out in *For the Common Good*, for a national government to perform its essential functions in support of market efficiency it must have jurisdiction over a national economy. Only when a strong, democratic government is able to set and enforce a necessary framework of rules for the market can the sovereign people hold the institutions of money accountable to the public interest. Eliminating national economic borders—a process that has been aggressively advanced by the structural adjustment programs of the World Bank and IMF and trade agreements negotiated under the General Agreement on Tariffs and Trade (GATT), the Asian Pacific Economic Community

DAVID C. KORTEN

(APEC), Maastricht, and the North American Free Trade Agreement (NAFTA), severely limits the ability of governments to set such a framework.

Whether intended or not, the consequence has been a step-by-step freeing of global corporations and financial institutions from public accountability for the impact of their actions on the living world. When considering the consequences, it is important to bear in mind that the consolidation of the world's national markets into a single borderless global economy has not come about as a consequence of inexorable historical forces. This consolidation has been accomplished through the intentional efforts of a small group of powerful decision makers whose view of reality is dominated by the imperatives of the world of money.[23]

CONDITIONS FOR MARKET EFFICIENCY IN THE PUBLIC INTEREST

The market is an important and useful human institution for meeting those needs to which it is suited. Market economies are most likely to serve the living-world interests of people when:

➤ They function as adjuncts to robust household and community economies that sustain values of cooperation, sharing, trust, and mutual obligation;

➤ They are primarily local in character, augmented by, rather than dependent on, trading relationships with more remote localities;

➤ The ownership of capital is local and most productive and commercial activities are carried out by small enterprises;

➤ Strong, democratically-accountable governments

set and enforce rules for the market's socially productive function; and,

➤ A strong and politically active civil society holds government accountable to the public interest as defined by engaged citizens.

When any of these conditions are not met, the market is prone to function in ways contrary to the human and natural interest. A globalized market tends to negate all of these conditions. The result is enormous social inefficiency and malfunction—as the world is now experiencing.

It is time to move beyond an economic model that is captive to the imperatives of the money world. The human future depends on finding more holistic approaches to dealing with poverty, unemployment, and social disintegration that give priority to meeting basic needs, restoring the bonds of community, and healing the planet. The idea is not to exclude the market or productive enterprise, but rather to assure that their function is consistent with the principles of equity, sustainability, and civic engagement.

RECLAIMING THE MARKET

The market theories of Adam Smith—which are widely invoked to support the argument that unregulated competitive markets are the most efficient form of economic organization—embody a number of critical assumptions. In particular, they assume that the market is comprised of small buyers and sellers and that the ownership of capital is local. Similarly, the trade theories of David Ricardo—which are invoked to show the universal benefits of free trade—embody the assumption that trade is between well defined national economies and that investment capital is confined within national borders. A borderless, unregulated global economy governed by massive flows of computerized money and gigantic stateless corporations negates most of the assumptions on which the classical theories of trade and the market economy are based.

Markets in just and sustainable societies must more closely approximate the conditions assumed by the classical economists. This will require a number of radical reforms, including breaking up the largest corporations through aggressive antitrust action, restoring economic boundaries to create public accountability, and redistributing wealth through progressive taxation and policies favoring local ownership of productive assets. Such actions depend on implementing political reforms to reduce the influence of big corporations and big money and restore meaning to the democratic principle of one person, one vote.

It may be necessary to establish in law that corporations—in contrast to the natural born people who own, manage, and work for them—have no inherent or inalienable human rights. The corporation is a public body created by government through the grant of a public charter to serve a public purpose. Natural rights belong to the living world, not the money world. The corporation is a creature of the money world. It has no rightful role in writing the rules governing its own conduct in relation to the living world.

Restoring economic and political power to people and communities is a necessary step toward achieving greater equity in the allocation of the earth's natural wealth both within and among nations. This will mean replacing the current commitment to economic globalization with a commitment to a global system of localized economies that rely primarily on local resources to serve local markets. Economic policies that favor distant corporations will need to be replaced with policies that favor smaller, locally owned businesses, especially those that are worker and community owned and that produce goods using sustainably harvested local resources to meet local needs. Trade rules will need to be rewritten with the goal of making it difficult for one group to pass the social and environmental costs of its own production onto others.

Tax policies will need to be radically reformed to provide greater incentive for things that should be encouraged—such as productive work—and reduce the costs of consumption related to meeting basic needs. Thus, taxes might be removed from basic incomes, basic consumption items, and productive investments that increase the ability to meet basic needs in socially and environmentally beneficial ways. These would be replaced by taxes on those things just and sustainable societies will need to discourage—such as incomes larger than necessary to support a modest sustainable lifestyle, advertising that encourages unnecessary consumption, concentrations of financial assets, speculative and other forms of extractive investment, pollution emissions, and unsustainable natural resource harvesting and extraction.

Some may argue that such measures will mean hardship for those who now enjoy the affluent lifestyles of consumer economies. They certainly will make it more difficult to lead a high consumption lifestyles that can neither be sustained nor equitably shared in our full world. Fortunately, however, it is entirely possible to achieve

DAVID C. KORTEN

both justice and sustainability while simultaneously improving the quality of living for nearly everyone.

IV. Material Foundations of Just and Sustainable Societies

The work of Alan Durning is useful in taking the first step toward operationalizing the principles of environmental sustainability and economic justice. Durning's analysis makes a rough division of the world into three socio-ecological classes: overconsumers, sustainers, and the excluded. The overconsumers—the people whose lifestyles are unsustainable in a full world—are the some 20 percent of the world's people who consume roughly 80 to 85 percent of the world's available natural wealth—those whose lives are organized around automobiles, airplanes, meat-based diets, and the use of wastefully packaged disposable products. The excluded, a corresponding 20 percent of the world's people, live in absolute deprivation.

SUPPORTING THE SUSTAINER CLASS

It is significant that roughly 60 percent of the world's people, though they face many hardships, are more or less meeting their basic needs in reasonably sustainable ways. We may refer to them as the world's sustainer class. Unfortunately, from a living-world perspective, the goal of economic policy almost everywhere is to increase the consumption of the overconsumers and turn sustainers into overconsumers. This commitment is backed by World Bank and IMF lending and by billions of dollars in corporate advertising expenditures encour-

aging people to buy things they might not otherwise realize they want. Public policy backs this commitment
with substantial investment in subsidies for overconsumer lifestyles—such as for airports, roads and parking
facilities—to the neglect of public transit, sidewalks, and
bicycle paths. As a consequence, the lives of those who
live sustainably become more difficult.

This suggests the need for a radical rethinking of public policy and market relationships. Rather than striv-
ing to increase the size and levels of consumption of the
overconsumer class, the goal should be to improve the
quality of living that a sustainer lifestyle affords and to
move both overconsumers and the excluded into the sustainer class. Cities have an especially important role to
play in this process because of the potentials offered by
high density human settlements to provide a high quality of living at a relatively low environmental cost.

The widespread belief that moving from an overconsumer to a sustainer lifestyle involves sacrifice and
hardship is in part a consequence of misplaced public priorities embraced over the past fifty years in the name of
development. All too often, these policies have elimi-
nated the support systems that afford sustainers a high
quality of living and replaced them with systems that
make life in the sustainer class more difficult—as when
roads used by cyclists are converted to thruways
reserved for cars.

While responsible individual choices have an important role in eliminating over-consumption, they are often
limited by public choices beyond the individual's control. This point is readily demonstrated with regard to
four major systems—urban space and transportation,
food and agriculture, materials, and energy. Each system

DAVID C. KORTEN

raises basic issues relating to how human settlements are organized and managed.

URBAN SPACE AND TRANSPORT

It is an insidious process as it leads to destroying natural habitat, paving over once productive agricultural lands, separating people from nature and each other by even greater distances, and increasing dependence on the automobile, which leads to still more traffic congestion. Per capita energy consumption skyrockets—both for transportation, and to heat and cool the detached, single-family dwellings in which suburbanites live. And people who cannot afford a car become socially and economically disadvantaged.

It is estimated that one to two billion hours a year are wasted due to traffic congestion in the largest U.S. cities. In Bangkok the average worker loses the equivalent of 44 working days a year sitting in traffic.[24] There is sound foundation for the conclusion of urban ecologists William Rees and Mark Roseland that, "Sprawling suburbs are arguably the most economically, environmentally, and socially costly pattern of residential development humans have ever devised."[25]

These destructive patterns can be reversed. In 1992, Groningen, a Dutch city of 170,000 people, dug up its city center motor ways and took a variety of steps to make the bicycle the main form of transport. As a consequence, business has improved, rents have increased, and the flow of people out of the city has been reversed. Local businesses that once fought any restraint on the automobile are now clamoring for more restraint.[26]

Few measures would do more to improve the quality of community life and the health of the environment than organizing human settlements to reduce dependence on the automobile. Actions to help accomplish this goal include: planning and controlling the use of urban space to increase urban density and the proximity of work, home, and recreation; restricting parking facilities; increasing taxes on gasoline; and investing in public transit and facilities for pedestrians and cyclists.

FOOD AND AGRICULTURE

Food and agriculture systems almost everywhere are being converted to chemical-intensive mechanized production involving long distance shipping and dependent on captive contract producers, migrant laborers paid bare subsistence wages, and large government subsidies paid to giant corporations. The system is well suited to the profitable mass production of standardized food products by global agribusiness corporations. It comes at the cost of depleting soils and aquifers, contaminating water with chemical runoff, driving out the small family farms that were long the backbone of rural communities, and burdening taxpayers with subsidies to big corporations. In return the consumer gets highly processed, wastefully packaged foods of dubious nutritional value contaminated with chemical residues. While the system keeps supermarkets filled, it features misleading nutritional claims, misleads consumers as to the actual cost of what they eat, strongly resists any effort to inform consumers regarding additives, synthetic hormones, and toxic residues they may be ingesting, and gives little option of choosing organically grown, unprocessed foods produced by local farmers.

Even adults intent on exercising healthful and responsible food choices seldom have any way of knowing whether the piece of fish they are about to buy was caught by huge trawlers sweeping the ocean bare with fine-mesh drift nets, or harvested by a local fisherman using environmentally responsible gear. They have no way of knowing whether a piece of meat is from an animal raised on properly managed natural rangelands, or on fragile lands from which tropical forests were recently cleared and fattened in feedlots on grain that might otherwise have fed hungry people. Nor is there any way to tell whether the cows that supplied a particular bottle of milk have been injected with artificial hormones when government gives in to the demands of the companies that produce the hormones to prohibit the labeling that would allow informed choice.

Those blessed with adequate money have access to a nearly limitless amount and variety of food products, leading them to conclude that the existing food and agricultural system is a modern miracle. However, the modern food and agriculture system—with its attendant concentration of land ownership—provides no options at all for those who cannot find a paying job other than subsisting on charity or scavenging scraps from the garbage of the more well to do.

There is a similar inequity with regard to dwindling and increasingly privatized water supplies. The competition for water is intensifying in much of the world—between countries, between agricultural and urban uses, and between rich and poor. In many cities the wealthy may enjoy the privilege of filling their swimming pools with subsidized municipal water for practically nothing, while the poor have no options other than to pay a high percentage of their meager incomes to private water vendors for water to drink, cook, and wash.

If the goal is to provide a good living for people, then the food and agriculture system must be transformed—much as human settlements and transportation systems must be transformed to optimize the use of land and water resources to meet the needs of an expanding population for a nutritionally adequate diet, fiber, and livelihoods—and it must be done in environmentally sustainable ways.

Food and agriculture systems appropriate to just and sustainable societies will most likely be based on intensively managed small family farms producing a diverse range of food, fiber, livestock, and energy products for local markets. Farming practices will use bio-intensive methods to maintain soil fertility, retain water, and control pests. The food system will be designed to limit, contain, and recycle contaminants—including the recycling of human wastes—and will depend primarily on renewable solar-generated energy sources, including animal power and bio-gas, for preparation, production, processing, storage, and transport.[27] Steps toward such a system will include agrarian reform to break up large agricultural holdings, providing adequate credit facilities for small farmers, creating farmer-based research and extension systems oriented to bio-intensive methods, requiring full and accurate labeling of food products, eliminating financial and environmental subsidies for agricultural chemicals, increasing the costs of food transport by eliminating energy and other transportation subsidies, and creating locally accountable watershed management authorities to coordinate measures for soil and water protection and regeneration.

Moving toward more localized food and agriculture systems and healthier, less fatty diets, will require

DAVID C. KORTEN

adjustments in eating habits. The sacrifices may be far less than one might assume and those that are real will be offset by the benefits of a fertile earth and vibrant and secure human communities populated by people with healthy bodies and minds nourished by wholesome, uncontaminated foods. The elements of this vision are technically and socially feasible. They simply require restructuring the relevant systems to align with the imperatives of the living world rather than those of the money world.

MATERIALS

The "garbage index" is one of our best sustainability indicators. In blunt terms, to achieve sustainability we must reduce to zero the amount of waste product permanently thrown away into the environment without possibility of natural recycling. Once taken from the ground, minerals and other nonbiodegradable resources must become a part of society's permanent capital stock and be recycled in perpetuity. This means organizing productive activities as closed systems. Even organic materials can be returned to the environment only in ways that assure they are readily absorbed back into the natural production system.

Important as it is, individual recycling is insufficient. Most of our waste is created in the process of producing the things we consume and is discarded long before it reaches us—far from our knowledge or control. Furthermore, we are simply not offered certain choices. For example, the market does not offer a choice of a daily newspaper printed on recycled paper using nontoxic, biodegradable ink. If we were offered the choice of subscribing to a newspaper without advertisements, it would be possible for those of us who would prefer such an option to save sixty to sixty-five percent of the newsprint consumed by the typical American households.[28] Unfortunately, the choice is not available.

According to the Worldwatch Institute "most materials used today are discarded after one use—roughly two thirds of all aluminum, three fourths of all steel and paper, and an even higher share of plastic."[29] This diminishes the quality of our physical environment as materials are mined and the resulting wastes and garbage are discarded. Furthermore, most people find themselves working extra hours at unsatisfying—if not unpleasant—jobs to pay for things that are intended all too quickly, to quite literally become garbage.

Recycling not only eliminates mining wastes and saves the habitat from which resources are otherwise extracted, it also saves large amounts of energy. It requires only a third as much energy to produce steel from scrap as it does to produce it from ore, while reducing air pollution by 85 percent and water pollution by 76 percent. Making newsprint from recycled paper takes 25 to 60 percent less energy than producing it from virgin wood pulp—while reducing air pollutants by 74 percent and water pollutants by 35 percent.

Reusing a produce is even better. Recycling the glass in a bottle reduces energy consumption by a third compared to making a new bottle. Cleaning and reusing the bottle itself can produce an energy saving of as much as 90 percent.[30]

Another positive approach is called life cycle product planning and responsibility, an idea pioneered in Germany, where government-mandated programs encourage manufacturers of automobiles and household appliances to assume responsibility for the disassembly, reuse, and recycling of their products. In addition to being environmentally sound, it relieves the consumer of the disposal burden at the end of the product's life.[31] Often, life cycle management involves lease arrangements in which the ownership remains with the manufacturer. Producers who know they will be responsible for end disposal have an incentive to design their products for both durability and ease of recycling.

A related, but less ambitious incentive to producers involves charging them a fee to cover the estimated public cost of eventual disposal. Governments might also mandate the use of standardized durable glass containers that can be reused many times simply by washing and relabeling.[32] Of course, many such measures are most easily implemented when production, consumption, and reuse takes place in the same local market— one of many reasons for favoring localized economies.

ENERGY

Plentiful supplies of fossil fuels—petroleum, coal, and natural gas—combined with extensive public subsidies for energy production have made energy unrealistically cheap to the end user. This has resulted in a number of destructive practices.

➤ Using capital intensive production methods that substitute energy for labor—adding to unemployment.

➤ Producing goods in low wage countries and shipping them thousands of miles to sell in affluent markets—a highly profitable, but in most instances social and environmentally destructive process that places competitive pressure on local communities to lower wages, environmental standards, and working conditions.

➤ Encouraging the use of energy inefficient forms of construction and transportation—which results in the rapid depletion of nonrenewable energy sources, destroys the human and animal habitats from which coal, oil, and natural gas are extracted, and contributes to pollution and global warming.

Energy efficiency and a transition to renewable energy sources are important priorities in the design of the built environment and in other technology choices made by just and sustainable societies. The appropriate choices include the use of insulation and the energy efficient design of buildings to take advantage of natural heating and cooling and the use of energy efficient lighting and appliances. Multi-family, multi-use buildings and row houses are more energy efficient than single family dwellings. Zoning to bring home, work, shopping, and recreation into close proximity facilitates walking and bicycling—reducing the need for both automobiles and public transportation. Increasing recycling and local self-reliance in production provides local employment opportunities and reduces transportation costs. Many such measures can be implemented in ways that both increase energy efficiency and improve the quality of living.

FROM JOBS TO LIVELIHOODS

Advocates of economic growth persistently argue that growth is essential to create needed jobs and eliminate poverty. However, much of the economic growth that creates jobs is destroying livelihoods—as when massive development projects displace millions of people

DAVID C. KORTEN

from their homes and the lands and waters from which they sustain themselves. This has created economic dependence on activities that are destructive of both the environment and the quality of our living.

Viewed from the perspective of the world of money it would appear that the environmental and quality of living loses are unavoidable costs of economic survival. Many of the changes required to create just and sustainable societies will indeed eliminate jobs and reduce the profits of major corporations. Certainly this would be one consequence of reducing dependence on the automobile. One job in six in the United States is linked to the auto industry. In Australia it is one in ten.[33] A significant reduction in automobile use would be devastating for the automobile, petroleum, chemical, steel, rubber, and road construction industries. Unemployment would skyrocket and stock prices would plummet. On the other hand, each of the related industries places devastating demands on the environment.

So long as we define our options in terms of the logic and imperatives of the money world, the dilemma seems irreconcilable. It is easily resolved, however, if addressed in terms of the logic and imperatives of the living world of people and nature. Jobs and consumption are constructs of the money world. The imperatives of the living world require a different approach to organizing economic activity—one in which livelihoods become the organizing construct.

Webster's New World Dictionary defines a job as "a specific piece or work, as in one's trade, or done by agreement for pay; anything one has to do; task; chore; duty."[34] It defines a livelihood as "a means of living or of supporting life."[35] A job is a source of money. A livelihood is a way of living. When we talk of jobs we evoke an image of people working in the plants and factories of global corporations and their contractors. When we speak of sustainable livelihoods we evoke images of people and communities engaged in meeting individual and collective needs in environmentally sustainable ways.

Just and sustainable societies will surely use money as a medium of exchange for many kinds of transactions and paid employment will be a source of livelihood for many people. However, many other transactions will be based on mutual caring relationships. And a great many people may be freed from wage employment to spend a consequential portion of their time in unpaid vocations performing services useful to the well-being of family, community, and society.

Rather than attempting to create new jobs at any cost, our priorities should be to eliminate many of those jobs that are harmful to the well-being of person and community, while creating more livelihood opportunities. Consider the possibilities. A great many of the jobs in the automobile, chemical, packaging, petroleum, advertising, marketing, financial, legal, and defense industries are neither satisfying nor life sustaining. In the latter category alone, 14 million workers are employed in the production of arms and another 30 million are employed by the world's military forces[36]—which in turn account for some 30 percent of all global environmental degradation.[37]

Imagine the possibilities. Instead of paying hundreds of millions of people sometimes outrageous amounts of money to do things that diminish the quality of our lives, we could just as well pay them a decent living wage to sit home and do nothing. Better yet, we could use the same money to pay them for truly useful work such as maintaining parks and commons areas, replanting forests, providing loving care and attention to children and the elderly, operating community markets and senior citizen centers, educating the young, cleaning up the environment, counseling drug addicts, providing proper care for the mentally ill, participating in community crime watches, organizing community social and cultural events, registering voters, doing public interest political advocacy, caring for community gardens, organizing community recycling programs, retrofitting homes for energy conservation, and participating in community musical groups. In addition, we might offer the presently over-worked more time for family life, recreation, quiet solitude, and the practice of disciplines and hobbies that keep mind and body physically, mentally, psychologically, and spiritually healthy.

Given the imperatives of the living world, it seems nearly inevitable that the just and sustainable societies of the twenty-first century will be organized to substantially reduce the use of automobiles, the release of toxic and nondegradable substances, the generation of garbage, and energy inefficiency. Most people will not consider it a great sacrifice to give up long commutes on crowded freeways, constant noise, job insecurity, gadgets they never use, clothes they seldom wear, unhealthy fatty diets, chemically contaminated fruits and vegetables, products that don't last, useless packaging, tiring business trips, energy inefficient homes and buildings, and armed conflicts. Not doing those things that are destructive will free up time to do essential work otherwise not done and for pursuits that give us greater satisfaction and scope for social, intellectual, and spiritual growth.

V. Social Foundations of Just and Sustainable Societies

> "Our village was prosperous. . . . The real foundation of our prosperity . . . was the deep and enduring sense of community that enabled us to make the best use of these resources. . . . We had all the things we needed—well-crafted, beautiful things that lasted a long time—but we did not do much 'consuming.'" — Eknath Easwaran, The Compassionate Universe[38]

Healthy families are the foundation of healthy communities, which in turn are the foundation of healthy societies. While they may take many forms—one mark of healthy families, communities, and societies is their capacity to nurture a dense fabric of caring relationships based on reciprocity, mutual trust, and cooperation.

SOCIAL CAPITAL AND THE HUMAN NEED FOR BONDING

Harvard University political scientist Robert Putnam refers to the bonding that characterizes a strong civil society as "social capital," and has shown its importance in a study of local government effectiveness in Italy. Beginning in 1970, Italy created twenty regional governments with identical formal structures. There were dramatic differences, however, in the local social, economic, political, and cultural contexts within which these structures were implanted. The localities ranged "from the pre-industrial to the post-industrial, from the devoutly Catholic to the ardently Communist, from the inertly feudal to the frenetically modern."[39]

In some localities the new government structures were "inefficient, lethargic, and corrupt." In others they were dynamic and effective, "creating innovative day care programs and job training centers, promoting investment and economic development, pioneering environmental standards and family clinics."

Putnam found only one set of indicators that consistently differentiated those localities in which the new structures produced positive results from those that did not. These were indicators of a strong and active civil society as measured by "voter turnout, newspaper readership, membership in choral societies and literary clubs, Lions Clubs and soccer clubs." Rich networks of nonmarket relationships built a generalized sense of trust and reciprocity—"social capital"—that increased the efficiency of human relationships in both market and governmental affairs.[40] A study by IBASE of a number of municipalities in Brazil has replicated Putnam's results.[41]

While competitive instincts form an important part of human nature, there is substantial evidence that it is a sub-theme to the more dominant theme of cooperation. According to cultural anthropologist Mary Clark, "The early human species could not have survived without the expanded social bonding between parent and offspring needed to protect helpless human infants[42]—a job that mothers alone could not accomplish. Social bonding to one's group was a biological necessity—for adults as well as infants." As with all species that depend on social bonding for their survival, there is strong reason to believe that humans evolved to belong and cooperate, as well as to compete.

The cultures of healthy societies maintain cooperation and competition in a state of dynamic, but balanced tension. Social bonding without competition leads to stagnation and a lack of innovation. Competition without social bonding leads to a violent anarchy. A dominance of money-world values has created a severe imbalance favoring competition over cooperation in our modern world.

Traditionally most of the productive and reproductive activities that provided people with their basic needs for food, shelter, clothing, child care, health care, education, physical security, and entertainment were carried out within the framework of the caring economy of family and community, largely outside of the market. A substantial portion of production/consumption activities took place within a single household or between people who related directly to one another. People met most of their needs through these nonmarket productive activities. In many societies, families and communities were the primary source of an individual's identity and livelihood and their importance provided a substantial incentive for people to invest in maintaining the social bonds of trust and obligation—the social capital—that is a necessary underpinning of any healthy society.

It is a fundamental, though often neglected fact, that social bonding is as essential to the healthy function of a modern society as it was to more traditional or tribal societies. Indeed, the market itself depends on the bonds of a well developed social capital to maintain the ethical structure, social stability, and personal security essential to its efficient function.

However, contemporary societies intent on money-world imperatives take little account of social capital and the means of its formation. Social capital finds no place in national income statistics by which money-centered societies define their well-being. It is undervalued by policy makers who count only monetized activities in the market economy as productive contributions to national output. Uncounted, the impact of economic policies on a society's social capital are neglected by decision makers. One need only ask a series of questions such as the following to arrive at a highly accurate estimate of the state of a locality's social capital and to appreciate the potential impact of economic policies on it.

➤ Do people prefer to shop in small local shops run by merchants they know by name, or in mega-shopping malls and large retail chain outlets? Do they favor the farmers' market or the supermarket?

➤ Are farms small, individually owned, and family operated? Or are they controlled by huge corporate enterprises and worked mainly by itinerant landless laborers?

➤ Are there local non-commercial print, radio, and television media where members of the community can express a diversity of ethnic, social, political, and cultural views? Or is all community news and need filtered through commercially controlled media?

➤ Do people devote their free time to Little League baseball, community gardens, local theater, community choirs, community centers, and school boards—or to watching commercial TV?

➤ Are there credit cooperatives and local banks committed to supporting local enterprise or only branches of large urban banks engaged in channeling local deposits into their global financial operations?

➤ Do residents consider the area their permanent home or are working and professional people largely itinerant?

➤ Do most households feel secure in their basic sustenance or do they depend for their survival on poorly paid temporary work?

➤ Are productive assets owned locally or by distant corporations?

➤ Are forests harvested selectively and sustainably by local firms to provide materials for local industry? Or are local forests stripped bare every 40 to 60 years by global corporations and the raw timber exported to distant lands?

The answers to such questions are powerful predictors of the sense of dignity, freedom, responsibility, prosperity, and security of local people; the extent to which relationships are characterized by trust, sharing, and cooperation—and even of the health of local ecosystems.

SOCIAL CONSEQUENCES OF MARKETIZATION

Another consequence of not counting nonwaged productive and reproductive work in economic statistics is that policy makers take little note of the fact that a considerable portion of the economic growth of recent decades has been achieved simply by shifting functions such as child care, health care, food preparation, entertainment, or the maintenance of physical security from household and community economies, where they are not counted in GNP, to the market economy, where they are.

Converting cooperative, nonmonetized relationships into competitive, monetized relationships does not in itself produce an evident improvement in the well-being of the individuals involved. It does, however, encourage greater competitiveness in relationships and increase the dependence of the individual on the market and the institutions of money. It also reduces the centrality of family and community life and leaves less time and energy to invest in family and community relationships. This, in turn, contributes to the erosion of a society's social capital.

It also has another rarely noted consequence. When family and community members work directly with and for one another in household and community economies there are no taxes, tax collectors and government regulators, management salaries, lawyers fees, stockholder dividends, middlemen, and other overhead expenses. The full value of the goods and services produced is shared and exchanged among those who engage in creating real value.[43] The result is an extraordinarily efficient use of resources to produce needed goods and services as there is virtually no overhead. In effect, in the money economy the producers, those who create real value, retain a lesser share of that value relative to those who perform unproductive overhead functions.

In many localities the market economy's overhead costs have become so high that even with two wage earners and longer work hours many households cannot now adequately meet needs once met quite satisfactorily through cooperative arrangements among household and community members. This compounds the problem of social capital erosion. Unable to find a job paying an adequate wage to support a family, marriage is indefinitely postponed. Mothers—irrespective of whether married or single—find paid employment is a necessity, not an option. In Northern countries without extended family or community self-help relationships, children are left at home with no adult supervision or are sequentially cared for by nannies, nurseries, day-care centers, and schools.

Parents—often a single impoverished female parent—are left with little time and energy or encouragement to do more than function as income earners and night guardians. The modern urban home is reduced to being little more than a place to sleep and watch television—if the household can afford one. Many reproductive functions are simply left unattended, as are many of the voluntary activities essential to the maintenance of community. Furthermore, even the less personalized, publicly funded social services that previously helped to fill the gap in the reproductive functions have been sharply curtailed in Southern countries by World Bank/IMF structural adjustment programs and in the North by right-wing extremists intent on reducing taxes and dismantling government. High rates of deprivation, depression, divorce, teenage pregnancy, violence, alcoholism and drug abuse, crime and suicide are among the more evident consequences in both high and low income countries.[44]

If public policy is to address these critical indicators of social breakdown, it must address their underlying economic and social causes.

GENDER BALANCE AND SOCIAL CAPITAL FORMATION

Just and sustainable societies require a solid foundation of social capital. While social capital is created by people—not governments—both public economic and social policies are needed that facilitate its creation. These policies must be informed by an acute gender awareness as gender is central to so many of the issues of social dysfunction. For example, the fact that public policy gives little importance to social capital is almost certainly related to the fact that historically social capital formation has been largely the responsibility of women—whose productive and reproductive functions have been likewise undervalued. The result has been both a serious distortion of policy priorities and an injustice to women.

The substantial increase in visibility of women's issues and their movement into the work place during the past ten to twenty years creates an impression that women are making substantial gains. In some respects they are. However, this is only part of the story. As a consequence of the current economic restructuring in many countries it is increasingly difficult for a household to survive without at least two full-time wage earners. The resulting stresses on the family account, in part, for the fact that growing numbers of households are headed by a single female. Consequently, more and more women find themselves the sole providers and caretakers for their children, a nearly unbearable burden in societies in which jobs are scarce, wages are low, women are paid less than men, and social services are being cut back in the name of fiscal responsibility. More than ever, women stand as the last line of defense against complete social disintegration—but with declining support in performing this essential function.

The injustice is compounded by laws and traditions that discriminate in favor of men with regard to land ownership and access to credit—including for housing construction. Even in two-parent households, in many cultures women have primary responsibility for the physical construction and maintenance of the dwelling. Women are similarly more likely than men to be denied access to the natural resources that are essential to many forms of livelihood creation. The fact that women are significantly under-represented in elected office limits attention to redressing the injustices.

A wide variety of actions are required to correct such distortions and begin the task of restoring the essential social fabric of civilized societies.

➤ Give adequate priority in economic policy to achieving a level of wages and public services—including clean water, education, health, and public transport—adequate for a household with children to live at a decent standard with the income from no more than the equivalent of one full-time paid job.

➤ Turn the structural adjustment policies of the World Bank and IMF on their head: 1) the development of adequate public services should have priority over the repayment of foreign loans; 2) the needs of local small enterprise producing for local markets should have precedence over the needs of global corporations seeking local export platforms; and 3) good wages and fair labor standards should be given more importance than opening domestic markets to foreign competitors that do not observe such standards.

➤ Extend to those who make careers of family and community service the same entitlements to social security and other public benefits extended to paid workers.

➤ Implement credible indicators of the health of the social capital stock and the social and economic contributions of unpaid work to assure that these receive public recognition and are visible to policy makers.

➤ Assure women equal rights of access to land,

DAVID C. KORTEN

credit, and construction materials for shelter and for their economic enterprises.

➤ Encourage greater political participation by women.

➤ Sustain a community media system where individual citizens and non-profit organizations can produce programs presenting their views, news, and cultures.

Elevating more women to positions of political leadership is especially important to the task of restoring the needed balance between the money world and the living world. Because of their long established nurturing roles outside the money economy, the lives of most women have been more closely linked to the living world. They are most often the creators and caretakers of the social capital of family and community, hence more likely than men to understand the imperatives of the living world. Finally, they suffer unequally from the dysfunctions of money-world institutions, which increases their understanding of those dysfunctions and heightens their commitment to correcting them.

The appropriate response to a disintegrating social fabric is not to restore women to their traditional subordinated family roles. Rather the goal should be to create new gender-balanced family and community structures that engage men and women equally in both reproductive and productive functions and in both paid and unpaid work.

ECONOMIC DEMOCRACY AND THE SOCIAL FABRIC

Advocates of the "free market" commonly argue that the market is the most democratic of institutions, because businesses prosper by responding to consumer choice. It is a disingenuous argument. Democracy is based on the principle of one person, one vote. The market functions on the principle of one dollar, one vote. Consequently, under conditions of unequal economic power, a society ruled by the market is a society ruled by those who have the most money—the antithesis of democracy. Further distortions result when huge global corporations acquire the power to manipulate cultural symbols and consumer demand through advertising and control of mass media. When tobacco companies set out to sell cigarettes to children they are not simply responding to an established demand, they are creating it.

The market is an important and useful human institution essential to the efficient function of modern societies. However, contrary to contemporary interpretations of Adam Smith, there is no magic that guides the unrestrained market in the public interest.

It is often forgotten that Adam Smith's classic treatise, *The Wealth of Nations*, explains how markets tend to favor the public good only under those conditions in which buyers and sellers are small, the ownership of capital is local, and there are no monopolies or trade secrets—conditions wholly different from those that prevail in our present global economy. Smith was a dedicated foe of large corporations, absentee ownership, trade secrets, and monopoly power. Unfortunately, he never dealt with the question of how to maintain the conditions under which the market achieves a socially optimal allocation of resources. We have since learned that this requires a strong hand from a democratic government held accountable to the public interest by a politically conscious and actively engaged civil society.

DAVID C. KORTEN

If Smith were alive today he would almost surely be an advocate of economic democracy, an economic system based on local worker ownership. There is a great need for a new kind of economic restructuring aimed at creating the conditions that Smith so accurately identified as the foundation of market efficiency in the public interest.

The global employment crisis is not so much a problem of too few jobs as it is a problem of an economic model that creates too much dependence on paid employment, pays too little to adequately support a family, encourages unnecessary consumption, and rewards people for doing things that are harmful while neglecting essential needs. It is instructive to remember that until the last ten to twenty years, most people—including the vast majority of women—have served society productively in essential unpaid work in the household/community economy. In many instances these societies had a stronger social fabric and offered their members a greater sense of personal security and fulfillment than do contemporary societies in which both men and women find themselves working long hours in paid employment to earn a bare subsistence wage. While many see the movement of women into the labor force as benefiting women by giving them greater choice, in far too many instances this has been more a matter of survival than one of expanded choice. Again, the goal should be to create societies that offer both women and men a greater choice of productive engagement in both paid work and in voluntary family and community work.

VI. Spiritual Foundations of Just and Sustainable Societies

At one point in time, paper money corresponded to units of gold which could be demanded of banks in exchange for the paper money. Today, the world of money is built on a pure abstraction. Objectively, money is nothing more than a substanceless and graceless icon of no intrinsic value—a simple number on a piece of paper, a coin, or in a computer. Yet its acquisition and replication have become a modern obsession. Which causes us to yield inordinate power to the institutions of money.

According to contemporary philosopher Joseph Needleman,

> In other times and places, not everyone has wanted money above all else; people have desired salvation, beauty, power, strength, pleasure, propriety, explanations, food, adventure, conquest, comfort. But now and here, money—not necessarily even the things money can buy, but money—is what everyone wants. The outward expenditure of mankind's energy now takes place in and through money.... Therefore, if one wishes to understand life, one must understand money in this present phase of history and civilization.[45]

What is the source of this seemingly irrational obsession? From what source does money—a mere number—derive its energy?

Joe Dominguez and Vicki Robin tell us that money derives its energy from our own spiritual energies. As they explain, "Money is something we choose to trade our life energy for. . . . Our allotment of time here on earth, the hours of precious life available to us. When

　　　　　　　　　　　DAVID C. KORTEN

we go to our jobs, we are trading our life energy for money. This truth, while simple, is profound."[46]

People chose to trade their energies for money because they are surrounded by advertising messages telling them that the fulfillment they seek is to be found in consuming the advertised products. Advertisers do not sell laundry soap, they sell acceptance, achievement, and personal worth. They do not sell automobiles, they sell power, freedom, and success—the opportunity to feel alive, connected, and free—that which people really want. Money is ceaselessly promoted as our ticket to the same things Needleman tells us people have wanted in other times and places.

Having defined ourselves in terms of money, we become entrapped in a downward spiral of increasing alienation from living, from our own spiritual nature. In the search for life we give money the power to destroy not only our own lives, but the rest of the living world as well.

Rather than teaching that the path to fulfillment is to experience living to the fullest through relationships with family, community, nature, and the living cosmos, a media dominated by money-world institutions continuously repeats a false promise: whatever one's longings, money and the sponsor's product are the path to instant gratification. Entranced by the siren song of the money world, we consistently undervalue the life energy that we put into obtaining money and overvalue the expected life energy gains from spending it.

The more we give our life energies over to money, the more power we yield to the institutions that control access to money and to the things that money will buy. Yielding such power serves well the corporate interest, because corporations are creatures of money. It serves poorly the human interest, because people are creatures of community, nature, and spirit.

Forced to reexamine who we are by the limits of the planet's ability to sustain the demands of our greed, we find ourselves confronted with a remarkable truth. Our pursuit of material abundance has created not abundance, but scarcity. By contrast, the pursuit of life brings a sense of social, spiritual, and even material abundance.

It is well demonstrated that people who experience an abundance of love in their lives rarely seek solace in compulsive, exclusionary personal acquisition. In contrast, no extreme of materialistic indulgence can ever be "enough" for the emotionally deprived as all the riches of the material world become insufficient to support the demands placed on them. Thus, a world starved of love becomes a world of material scarcity. In contrast, a world with abundant love is also a world of material abundance.

When we are socially whole and experience the caring support of community, thrift is a natural part of a full and disciplined life. That which is sufficient to one's needs brings a fulfilling sense of nature's abundance.

Overconsumer societies are built around financial pursuits. Just and sustainable societies are built on a community's social, ethnic, cultural and spiritual foundations.

VII. Civic Engagement for Transformational Change

There are signs throughout the world of a political and spiritual awakening of civil society to the reality that

DAVID C. KORTEN

national and global institutions are pursuing agendas at odds with the needs of people and other living things. Countless citizen initiatives prompted by this awakening are coalescing into a global political movement for transformational change. The emergent social forces find expression in local initiatives aimed at regenerating local economies, ecosystems, and communities. For example, the United Nations Conference on Environment and Development (UNCED) inspired initiatives in more than 3,000 communities around the world to create local Agenda 21s.

WITHHOLDING LEGITIMACY, RECLAIMING RESPONSIBILITY

As people reclaim responsibility, they are also withdrawing the legitimacy from the institutions that have abandoned them, reasserting their basic rights over local resources, and demanding greater public accountability from governments and global corporations. They are also reaching out to form new alliances, both nationally and internationally, with those engaged in similar initiatives. Most of these initiatives are peaceful. Some are not.

January 1, 1994 was inaugural day for the North American Free Trade Agreement (NAFTA), which guaranteed the rights of money, goods, and companies to move freely between Mexico, Canada, and the United States without interference from national governments or borders. Business leaders throughout North America were elated by the expanded opportunities to produce cheaply in Mexico on the backs of low paid workers and an unprotected environment while selling dearly in the affluent markets of the United States and Canada. The indigenous peoples of Chiapas State in southeastern Mexico, however, correctly recognized the NAFTA agreement as an extension of economic forces that for generations had step-by-step deprived them of their lands and their livelihoods. In response they launched an armed rebellion against the Mexican government. Their battle cry—"*Basta!*" (Enough!)—was picked up by popular movements all across Mexico and resonated around the world.

Mexican political analyst Gustavo Esteva pronounced the Chiapas rebellion the "first revolution of the twenty-first century." Revolutions of the twentieth century were contests for state power. By contrast, the Chiapas people struggled for greater local autonomy, economic justice, and political rights within the borders of their own communities.[47] They called on their fellow Mexicans not to take up arms against the state, but rather to join in a broad social movement to liberate local spaces everywhere from political and economic forces that recognize no accountability to people or place—a struggle likely to dominate much of the politics of the 21st century.

Elsewhere in North America middle class Canadians have taken up a similar cry. Fed up with a conservative government that seemed to place the rights of global corporations ahead of the rights of Canadian people and communities, they rallied in their October 1993 national election to vote out all but two members of the ruling Tory party from their parliament. It was one of the most sweeping repudiations of a democratically elected government in history. Once seated, the new Liberal party government went on to carry out essentially the same policies as the government the electorate had voted out. It led many Canadians to believe that global economic interests had usurped control over their government and

DAVID C. KORTEN

the Canadian economy. A citizen organization, the Council of Canadians, was formed to oppose these forces. When NAFTA came into force at the beginning of 1994, the Council launched an initiative to develop a "Citizens' Agenda for Canada" to define the kind of society that Canadians want for themselves and their children. By 1997 the Council had reached 100,000 members and continued to grow at a rapid pace.

In Brazil a very different citizen initiative was underway to address similar forces. Citizenship Action Against Misery and for Life—a grassroots hunger movement spearheaded by Herbert "Betinho" de Souza of IBASE—sought to transform national politics. Betinho had emerged as a public hero of a successful Brazilian citizen movement that led to the impeachment in 1993 of president Fernando Collor for gross corruption. Once the new government was installed, Betinho decided to capitalize on his reputation and the sense of civic empowerment instilled by the success of the impeachment campaign to mobilize Brazilians behind a national commitment to end the perpetual hunger of 32 million Brazilians who lived on incomes of less than $120 a year. Most Brazilians readily accepted Betinho's assessment that this situation was a national disgrace in a country with one of the world's most modern and dynamic economies.[48] Responding to Betinho's call, some 2.8 million Brazilians organized themselves into neighborhood hunger committees comprised of workers, students, housewives, business persons, artists, and others. As they engaged the task of ending hunger in their respective neighborhoods they were encouraged to ask why so many people could find no opportunity in the midst of a thriving economy. A 1994 survey revealed that roughly a third of Brazil's adult population contributed personally to the campaign in one way or another.[49]

The movement's participants are encouraged to reflect on the act of befriending and improving the life of a hungry person as both a political and a spiritual experience and as a source of insight into the causes of the dysfunctions of Brazilian society. Facilitated through media presentations and local meetings, citizens are led to a growing awareness of the dynamics of inequality and exclusion that flow from the concentration of economic power in a few giant corporations.

In country after country people are demonstrating that they are no longer willing to leave it to mainstream political parties and special interest lobbyists to set the terms of the public policy debate. They are acting to reclaim their basic rights and sovereignty as citizens to recreate their societies in ways that better respond to their needs and aspirations.

GLOBALIZING CIVIL SOCIETY

Many citizen groups are reaching out to form national and international alliances committed to transformational changes aimed at addressing root causes of the growing global crisis. An emergent social movement is coalescing around a shared vision of a world of diverse cultures and just and sustainable communities living in balance with the natural world and joined in cooperative endeavor—not by a global economy ruled by powerful corporations—but by an awareness of the underlying interdependence of the living world. This movement celebrates the emergence of a new global awareness and sense of solidary that is joining people from every part

DAVID C. KORTEN

of the planet in the task of creating a new global civilization grounded in peace and cooperation.

This movement gained substantial impetus from the NGO Forum of the United Nations Conference on Environment and Development (UNCED) held in Rio in 1992. This Forum brought together civil society organizations from all around the world to negotiate a series of citizen treaties for creating a just and sustainable world. It was here that the emergent movement began to become more consciously aware of itself as participants from widely diverse backgrounds came to realize the extent to which they shared common values and aspirations. The basic elements of this emergent consensus, as revealed through the discussions of the UNCED NGO Forum and the commitments that flowed from them, were recorded in *The People's Earth Declaration*.[50]

International women's organizations have taken a central leadership role in carrying this process forward through the NGO Forums of UNCED and subsequent UN conferences. The movement is now going through a transition, moving beyond the critique of failing institutions to building practical policy agendas for the human future. Here again women are in the lead, moving beyond more traditional gender politics to work on creating an inclusive vision of a world that will provide a better future for everyone—with support and encouragement from the United Nations Womens' Organization (UNIFEM).

The needed rethinking of human institutions will not be accomplished in conventional international conferences dominated by the institutions that have created our crisis. We must look for creative new approaches to advancing realization of a citizen-led vision of the human future. One possibility might be to convene the world's first truly global conference in the year 2000. Instead of limiting participation to those able to travel to one of the world's major cities, it might involve thousands of simultaneous, independently organized citizen gatherings all over the world in which people share their experiences, hopes, and commitments toward creating just and sustainable societies for the third millennium.

A major focus might be on neighborhood, village, and municipal level gatherings that bring people together in the places where they live. Others would be national, regional, and international. All would be meetings of people meeting in their capacity as fellow human beings rather than as representatives of particular groups and institutions. Every locality and participating organization would be responsible for its own events. The various gatherings would be linked into a global dialogue and celebration through a variety of electronic media including video, radio, and the Internet. Such a process would itself embody an approach to citizen engagement in local, national and global governance consistent with the democratic ideal of citizen sovereignty.

It is time for we the people of the world to work together as self-empowered citizens of a small and suffering planet to create just and sustainable societies dedicated to bringing our species into balance with itself and the planet. To do so we will need to reclaim the power we have yielded to institutions that no longer serve the human interest and to create new institutions dedicated to the premise that all power flows from the will and aspirations of the sovereign people. As the Zapatistas have taught us, the challenge is ours and the time is now.

DAVID C. KORTEN

Dr. David C. Korten is a founder and board chair of the Positive Futures Network, publishers of *Yes! A Journal of Positive Futures*, author of *When Corporations Rule the World*, and president of the People-Centered Development Forum. He is currently working on a book tentatively titled *Envisioning a Post-Corporate World*.

Appreciation is expressed to the following for their useful critical comments and inputs: Peggy Antrobus, Jeffrey Barber, Gerald Barney, Susan Davis, Anwar Fazal, Noeleen Heyzer, Frances Korten, Carolyn Pezzullo, Barry Pinsky, George Porter, Atila Roque, and David Satterthwaite. The opinions expressed are solely those of the author.

MORE INFORMATION

When Corporations Rule the World. The themes developed in this paper are elaborated in *When Corporations Rule the World*, copublished by Kumarian Press, 630 Oakwood Ave., Suite 119, West Hartford, CT 06110-1529, U.S.A., phone (203) 953-0214 / fax (203) 953-8589; and Berrett-Koehler Publishers, 155 Montgomery Street, San Francisco, CA 94104-4109, U.S.A., phone (415) 288-0260 / fax (415) 362-2512.

The Positive Futures Network publishers of *Yes! A Journal of Positive Futures*, P.O. Box 10818, Bainbridge Island, WA 98110-0818, U.S.A., phone (206) 842-0216; e-mail: yes@futurenet.org; http://www.futurenet.org

The People-Centered Development Forum (PCD-Forum), 14 E. 17th St., New York, NY 10003, U.S.A.; e-mail: pcdf@igc.apc.org.; http://iisd1.iisd.ca/pcdf

NOTES

1. This discussion of money versus living world imperatives is inspired by the observation of <u>Lester Brown in the Worldwatch</u> Institute's 1991 State of the World report that the world is divided between those whose view of the world is shaped by financial and economic indicators and those whose view is shaped by environmental indicators.

2. The United Nations High Commissioner for Refugees, *The State of the World's Refugees*(New York: Penguin Books: 1993).

3. Lester R. Brown and Hal Kane, *Full House: Reassessing the Earth's Population Carrying Capacity* (New York: W.W. Norton & Co., 1994).

4. "Executive Pay: The Party Ain't Over Yet," *Business Week*, April 26, 1993, pp. 56-62; and "That Eye-Popping Executive Pay: Is Anybody Worth This Much?" *Business Week*, April 25, 1994, pp. 52-58.

5. Sarah Anderson and John Cavanagh, "*The Top 200: The Rise of Global Corporate Power,*" Institute for Policy Studies, Washington, D.C., September 1996.

6. "A Survey of Multinationals: Everybody's Favourite Monsters," *The Economist*, March 27, 1993, special supplement, p. 6.

7. Asset figures for commercial banks and financial companies are from *Hoover's Handbook of World Business* (Austin, Texas: The Reference Press, 1993), pp. 68 & 72.

8. "A Survey of Multinationals," op. cit., p. 17

9. Stephanie Strom, "Mergers for Year Approach Record," *The New York Times*, October 31, 1995, p. A-1.

10. Richard J. Barnet and John Cavanagh, *Global Dreams: Imperial Corporations and the New World Order* (New York: Simon & Schuster, 1994), pp. 325-329; and *The Washington Post*, May 3, 1995, p. F-1.

11. An interview with Christopher Whalen, chief financial officer for Legal Research International, by Russell Mokhiber, *Corporate Crime Reporter*, January 19, 1995.

12. "The World's Wealthiest People," *Forbes*, July 5, 1993, p.66; and "The Billionaires," *Forbes*, July 18, 1995, pp. 194-95.

13. Anthony DePalma, "Mexicans Ask How Far Social Fabric Can Stretch," *The New York Times*, March 12, 1995, p. A-1.

14. Herman Daly, "Towards Some Operational Principles of Sustainable Development," *Ecological Economics*, Vol. 2, 1990, 1-6.

15. William E. Rees and Mathis Wackernagel, "Ecological Footprints and Appropriated Carrying Capacity: Measuring the Natural Capital Requirements of the Human Economy," in A-M-M Jannson, M. Hammer, C. Folke, R. Costanza (eds.) *Investing in Natural Capital: The Ecological Economics Approach to Sustainability* (Washington D.C.: Island Press, 1994), pp. 362-390 (p. 382).

16. Ibid., pp. 362-390 (p. 374).

17. Manus van Brakel and Maria Buitenkamp, "Sustainable Netherlands: A Perspective for Changing Northern Lifestyles," Milieudefensie, Damrak 26, 1012 LJ Amsterdam, Netherlands, May 1992.

DAVID C. KORTEN

18. Alex Hittle, "The Dutch Challenge: A Look at How the Untied States' Consumption must change to Achieve Global Sustainability," Washington, DC: Friends of the Earth, May 1994.

19. Brakel and Buitenkamp, op. cit.

20. David Pimental, Rebecca Harman, Matthew Pacenza, Jason Percarsky, and Marcia Pimentel, "Natural Resources and an Optimal Human Population," *Population and Environment, Volume 14, Number 5*, May 1994, p. 364

21. Ibid., p. 363

22. United Nations Centre for Human Settlements and the International Labour Office, *Shelter Provisions and Employment Generation* (Nairobi: United Nations Centre for Human Settlements (Habitat); and Geneva: International Labour Organization, 1995).

23. See David C. Korten, *When Corporations Rule The World*, (West Hartford, CT: Kumarian Press and San Francisco: Berrett-Koehler, 1995), pp. 121-181.

24. Statistics are reported by Marcia D. Lowe, "Reinventing Transport," in Lester R. Brown, et al., *State of the World 1994* (New York: W. W. Norton, 1994), pp. 81-98 (pp. 82-84) from a study by the United State Federal Highway Commission. For further discussion see Engwicht, ibid., pp. 138-144.

25. William E. Rees and Mark Roseland, "From Urban Sprawl to Sustainable Human Communities," *PCDForum Column #54*, June 25, 1993.

26. Nicholas Albery, Matthew Mezey, and Peter Ratcliffe (eds), *Social Innovations: A Compendium* (London: The Institute for Social Innovations), pp. 92-93.

27. Application of these concepts to villages in India is developed in detail in Anil Agarwal and Sunita Narain, *Towards Green Villages: A Strategy for Environmentally Sound and Participatory Rural Development* (New Dehli: Centre for Science & Environment, 1989).

28. Alan Thein Durning and Ed Ayres, "The Story of a Newspaper," *World Watch*, November/December 1994, pp. 30-32.

29. Lester R. Brown, Christopher Flavin, & Sandra Postel, *Saving the Planet: How to Shape an Environmentally Sustainable Economy* (New York: W.W. Norton, 1991), p.65.

30. Ibid., p. 65.

31. Ibid., p. 68.

32. Ibid., p. 70.

33. Robyn Williams in the Foreward to Engwicht, op. cit.

34. *Webster's New World Dictionary, second college edition* (New York: Simon & Schuster, 1980), p. 759

35. Ibid., p. 827.

36. The armed forces and defense worker estimates are from *UNDP, Human Development Report 1994* (New York: Oxford, 1994) pp. 47 and 60.

37. Michael Renner, "Assessing the Military's War on the Environment,"

in Lester R. Brown, et al., *State of the World 1991* (New York: W.W. Norton, 1991), p. 139.

38. Eknath Easwaran, *The Compassionate Universe: The Power of the Individual to Heal the Environment* (Tomales, CA: Nilgiri Press, 1989), pp. 73-74.

39. Robert D. Putnam, "The Prosperous Community: Social Capital and Public Affairs," *The American Prospect, Number 13*, Spring 1993, pp. 1-8. (p. 2).

40. Ibid., pp. 1-8 (p. 2).

41. Atila Roque, personal communication to the author, August 3, 1995.

42. Mary E. Clark, "The Backward Ones," *PCDForum Column #51*, The People-Centered Development Forum, New York, NY June 25, 1993.

43. Edgar Cahn and Jonathan Rowe, *Time Dollars* (Emmaus, Pennsylvania: Rodale Press, 1992).

44. Clarence Shubert, "Creating People-Friendly Cities," *PCDForum Column #72*, April 5, 1994.

45. Jacob Needleman, *Money and the Meaning of Life* (New York: Doubleday, 1991), p.40-42.

46. Joe Dominguez and Vicki Robin, *Your Money or Your Life: Transforming Your Relationships with Money and Achieving Financial Independence* (New York: Viking, 1992), p. 54.

47. Gustavo Esteva, Proceso, February 14 as quoted by "Chiapas and the Americas," *The Nation*, March 28, 1994, p. 404; and Neil Harvey, Rebellion in Chiapas: Rural Reforms, Campesino Radicalism, and the Limits to Salinismo, Transformation of Rural Mexico Series, Number 5, Ejido Reform Research project, Center for U.S.-Mexican Studies, University of California, San Diego, California, 1994, p.1.

48. "Hungry," *The Economist*, July 10, 1993.

49. Further information on *Action of Citizenship Against Misery and for Life* is available from Brazilian Institute for Social and Economic Analyses (IBASE), rua Vicente de Souza, 29-Botafogo, 22251 Rio de Janeiro/RJ, Brazil, Fax (55-21-) 286-0541.

50. For text of *The People's Earth Charter* see Appendix to David C. Korten, *When Corporations Rule the World* (West Hartford, CT: Kumarian Press and San Francisco: Berrett-Koehler, 1995)